Table of Contents

Introduction 3
   Multiple Sclerosis (MS) 4
   Symptoms Of MS 4
   Types Of Multiple Sclerosis 9
   Causes of Multiple Sclerosis (MS) 14
   Triggers Of MS Symptoms 19
   Tests For Multiple Sclerosis 20
   Multiple Sclerosis (MS) Treatments 28
Living With MS 36
   Effects Of MS 37
   Prognosis For People With MS 38
   MS and Diet 39
   Multiple Sclerosis Diet 44
   Foods To Eat 45
   Foods To Avoid 52
Special Diets 54
   Paleo diet 55
   Swank diet 56
Recipes 57
   Roasted Chicken Breast With Garlic Cloves 57
   Bell Peppers And Turkey Roll 58
   Wild Smoked Salmon Roll 59

Radishes With Hazelnut Sour Cream 60
Apple And Almond Butter 61
Cottage Cheese, Raisins, And Walnuts 61
Sardines With Edamame 62
Apple And Pear Minestrone 62
Baked Apples With Cranberries 63
Acai And Almond Milk Popsicle 64
Red Fruits Compote 65
Grilled Mango And Almonds 66
Peach With Apricot Coulis 67
Strawberries And Spinach Smoothie 68
Spring Fruit Salad With White Tea 69
Winter Fruit Salad 70
Melon Soup 70

Introduction

There is no evidence that a specific diet can prevent, treat or cure multiple sclerosis (MS). Some special diets can actually be harmful because they contain too much of certain vitamins or not enough of others. Make sure you talk to your doctor before making significant changes to your diet. Overall, people with MS need a balanced, low-fat and high-fiber diet. Unprocessed or naturally processed foods are preferred to processed foods. This is similar to the Mediterranean diet, and the same healthy diet that's recommended for the general population. Also consider limiting alcohol as much as possible. Some research suggests that a diet low in saturated fats and supplemented with omega-3 fatty acids may benefit people with MS. But these results haven't been confirmed by large-scale studies. However, it's recommended that people with MS limit animal-based fats. Instead, opt for fish and nut-based fat sources such as olive oil, avocado oil and almond butter, which are rich in omega-3s. Researchers are also investigating a link between vitamin D and biotin — a form of vitamin B also known as vitamin H — on multiple sclerosis disease activity. These studies are in the very early stages. Still, it's recommended that people with MS keep vitamin D levels in the upper range of normal.

Multiple Sclerosis (MS)

Multiple sclerosis (MS) is a chronic illness involving your central nervous system (CNS). The immune system attacks myelin, which is the protective layer around nerve fibers. This causes inflammation and scar tissue, or lesions. This can make it hard for your brain to send signals to the rest of your body.

Symptoms Of MS

Multiple sclerosis (MS) is a progressive, immune-mediated disorder. That means the system designed to keep your body healthy mistakenly attacks parts of your body that are vital to everyday function. The protective coverings of nerve cells are damaged, which leads to diminished function in the brain and spinal cord. MS is a disease with unpredictable symptoms that can vary in intensity. While some

people experience fatigue and numbness, severe cases of MS can cause paralysis, vision loss, and diminished brain function. Common early signs of multiple sclerosis (MS) include:
- vision problems
- tingling and numbness
- pains and spasms
- weakness or fatigue
- balance problems or dizziness
- bladder issues
- sexual dysfunction
- cognitive problems

Vision problems

Visual problems are one of the most common symptoms of MS. Inflammation affects the optic nerve and disrupts central vision. This can cause blurred vision, double vision, or loss of vision. You may not notice the vision problems immediately, as degeneration of clear vision can be slow. Pain when you look up or to one side also can accompany vision loss. There are variety of ways to cope with MS-related vision changes.

Tingling and numbness

MS affects nerves in the brain and spinal cord (the body's message center). This means it can send conflicting signals around the body. Sometimes, no signals are sent. This results in numbness. Tingling sensations and numbness are one of the most common warning signs of MS. Common sites of numbness include the face, arms, legs, and fingers.

Pain and spasms

Chronic pain and involuntary muscle spasmsare also common with MS. One study, according to the National MS Society, showed that half of people with MS had chronic pain. Muscle stiffness or spasms (spasticity) are also common. You might experience stiff muscles or joints as well as uncontrollable, painful jerking movements of the extremities. The legs are most often affected, but back pain is also common.

Fatigue and weakness

Unexplained fatigue and weakness affect about 80 percent of people in the early stages of MS. Chronic fatigue occurs when nerves deteriorate in the spinal column. Usually, the fatigue appears suddenly and lasts for weeks before improving. The weakness is most noticeable in the legs at first.

Balance problems and dizziness

Dizziness and problems with coordination and balance can decrease the mobility of someone with MS. Your doctor may refer to these as problems with your gait. People with MS often feel lightheaded, dizzy, or as if their surroundings are spinning (vertigo). This symptom often occurs when you stand up.

Bladder and bowel dysfunction

A dysfunctional bladder is another symptom occurring in up to 80 percent of people with MS. This can include frequent urination, strong urges to urinate, or inability to hold in urine. Urinary-related symptoms are often manageable. Less often, people with MS experience constipation, diarrhea, or loss of bowel control.

Sexual dysfunction

Sexual arousal can also be a problem for people with MS because it begins in the central nervous system — where MS attacks.

Cognitive problems

About half of people with MS will develop some kind of issue with their cognitive function. This can include:
- memory problems
- shortened attention span
- language problems
- difficulty staying organized

Depression and other emotional health problems are also common.

Changes in emotional health

Major depression is common among people with MS. The stresses of MS can also cause irritability, mood swings, and a condition called pseudobulbar affect. This involves bouts of uncontrollable crying and laughing. Coping with MS symptoms, along with relationship or family issues, can make depression and other emotional disorders even more challenging.

Other symptoms

Not everyone with MS will have the same symptoms. Different symptoms can manifest during relapses or attacks. Along with the symptoms mentioned on the previous slides, MS can also cause:
- hearing loss
- seizures
- uncontrollable shaking
- breathing problems
- slurred speech
- trouble swallowing

Types Of Multiple Sclerosis

Multiple sclerosis (MS) is thought to be an autoimmune, inflammatory disease affecting the central nervous system and peripheral nerves. The cause remains unknown, but some studies indicate a link between the Epstein Barr Virus, while others indicate environmental factors, a lack of vitamin D, or parasites as a stimulus of the persistent immune response in the central nervous system. It can be unpredictable and, in some cases, disabling. But not all forms of MS are the same. To help distinguish between the different types of the condition, the National Multiple Sclerosis Society (NMSS) identified four distinct categories. To accurately define the different forms of MS, in 1996, the NMSS surveyed a group of scientists who specialized in MS patient care and research. After analyzing the scientists' responses, the organization categorized the condition into four primary types. These course definitions were updated in 2013 to reflect advances in research. They are:

• clinically isolated syndrome (CIS)

• relapsing-remitting MS (RRMS)

• primary-progressive MS (PPMS)

• secondary-progressive MS (SPMS)

The four categories defined by the NMSS are now relied upon by the medical community at large and create a common language for diagnosing and treating MS. The categories' classifications are based on how far the disease has progressed in each patient.

Clinically isolated syndrome

Clinically isolated syndrome (CIS) is a single episode of neurologic symptoms that lasts 24 hours or more. Your symptoms cannot be tied to fever, infection, or other illness. They're the result of inflammation or demyelination in the central nervous system. You might have only one symptom (monofocal episode) or several (multifocal episode). If you have CIS, you may never experience another episode. Or this episode could be your first MS attack. If an MRI detects brain lesions similar to those found in people with MS, there's a 60 to 80 percent chance you'll have another episode and a diagnosis of MS within a few years. At this time, you might have a diagnosis of MS if an MRI detects older lesions in a different part of your central nervous system. That would mean you've had a previous attack, even if you weren't aware of it.

Relapsing-remitting MS

The most common type is relapsing-remitting MS (RRMS). According to the NMSS, approximately 85 percent of people with MS have this type at the

time of diagnosis. When you have RRMS you may experience:
- clearly defined relapses or flare-ups that result in episodes of intensive worsening of your neurologic function
- partial or complete remissions or recovery periods after the relapses and between attacks when the disease stops progressing
- mild to severe symptoms as well as relapses and remissions that last for days or months

Progressive types of MS

While the vast majority of people with MS have the RRMS form, some are diagnosed with a progressive form of the disease: primary-progressive MS (PPMS) or secondary-progressive MS (SPMS). Each of these types indicates that the disease continues to worsen without improvement.

Primary-progressive MS

This form of MS progresses slowly yet steadily from the time of its onset. Symptoms stay at the same level of intensity without decreasing, and there are no remission periods. In essence, patients with PPMS experience a fairly continuous worsening of their condition. However, there can be variations in the rate of progression over the course of the disease — as well as the possibility of minor improvements (usually temporary) and occasional plateaus in symptom progression. The NMSS estimates that approximately 15 percent of people with MS have PPMS at the onset of the condition.

Secondary-progressive MS

SPMS is more of a mixed bag. Initially, it may involve a period of relapsing-remitting activity, with symptom flare-ups followed by recovery periods. Yet the disability of MS doesn't disappear between cycles. Instead, this period of fluctuation is followed by a steady worsening of the condition. People with SPMS may experience minor remissions or plateaus in their symptoms, but this isn't always the case. Without treatment, about half of people with RRMS go on to develop SPMS within a decade.

Type casting

Early MS can be challenging for doctors to diagnose. As such, it can be helpful to understand the characteristics and symptoms of MS at the time of initial diagnosis — particularly since the vast majority of people with the disease exhibit characteristics of relapsing-remitting MS. Although MS currently has no cure, it isn't normally fatal. In fact, most people who have MS never become severely disabled, according to the NMSS. Identifying MS early at the relapsing-remitting stage can help ensure prompt treatment to avoid developing more progressive forms of the illness.

Causes of Multiple Sclerosis (MS)

Multiple sclerosis (MS) is a progressive neurological disease that can affect the central nervous system (CNS). Every time you take a step, blink, or move your arm, your CNS is at work. Millions of nerve cells in the brain send signals throughout the body to control these processes and functions:

• movement
• sensation

- memory
- cognition
- speech

Nerve cells communicate by sending electrical signals via nerve fibers. A layer called the myelin sheath covers and protects these fibers. That protection ensures that each nerve cell properly reaches its intended target. In people with MS, immune cells mistakenly attack and damage the myelin sheath. This damage results in the disruption of nerve signals. Damaged nerve signals can cause debilitating symptoms, including:

- walking and coordination problems
- muscle weakness
- fatigue
- vision problems

MS affects everyone differently. The severity of the disease and the types of symptoms vary from person to person. There are different types of MS, and the cause, symptoms, progression of disability may vary. The exact cause of MS is unknown. However, scientists believe that four factors may play a role in the development of the disease.

Cause 1: Immune system

MS is considered an immune-mediated disease: The immune system malfunctions and attacks the CNS. Researchers know that the myelin sheath is directly affected, but they don't know what triggers the immune system to attack the myelin. Research into which immune cells are responsible for the attack is ongoing. Scientists are seeking to uncover what causes these cells to attack. They're also searching for methods to control or stop the progression of the disease.

Cause 2: Genetics

Several genes are believed to play a role in MS. Your chance of developing MS is slightly higher if a close relative, such as a parent or sibling, has the disease. According to the National Multiple Sclerosis Society, if one parent or sibling has MS, the chances of getting the disease are estimated to be around 2.5 to 5 percent in the United States. The chances for an average person are approximately

0.1 percent. Scientists believe that people with MS are born with a genetic susceptibility to react to certain unknown environmental agents. An autoimmune response is triggered when they encounter these agents.

Cause 3: Environment

Epidemiologists have seen an increased pattern of MS cases in countries located farthest from the equator. This correlation causes some to believe that vitamin D may play a role. Vitamin D benefits immune system function. People who live near the equator are exposed to more sunlight. As a result, their bodies produce more vitamin D. The longer your skin is exposed to sunlight, the more your body naturally produces the vitamin. Since MS is considered an immune-mediated disease, vitamin D and sunlight exposure may be linked to it.

Cause 4: Infection

Researchers are considering the possibility that bacteria and viruses may cause MS. Viruses are known to cause inflammation and a breakdown of myelin. Therefore, it's possible that a virus could trigger MS. It's also possible that the bacteria or virus that have similar components to brain cells trigger the immune system to mistakenly identify normal brain cells as foreign and destroy them. Several bacteria and viruses are being investigated to determine if they contribute to the development of MS. These include:

- measles viruses
- human herpes virus-6, which leads to conditions such as roseola
- Epstein-Barr virus

Other risk factors

Other risk factors may also increase your chances of developing MS. These include:

- Sex. Women are at least two to three times more likely to develop relapsing-remitting multiple sclerosis (RRMS) than men. In the primary-progressive (PPMS) form, numbers of men and women are approximately equal.
- Age. RRMS usually affects people between the ages of 20 and 50. PPMS usually occurs approximately 10 years later than other forms.

- Ethnicity. People of northern European descent are at highest risk of developing MS

Triggers Of MS Symptoms

There are several triggers that people with MS should avoid.

Stress

Stress can trigger and worsen MS symptoms. Practices that help you reduce and cope with stress can be beneficial. Add de-stressing rituals to your day, such as yoga or meditation.

Smoking

Cigarette smoke can add to the progression of MS. If you smoke, look into effective methods of quitting. Avoid being around secondhand smoke.

Heat

Not everyone sees a difference in symptoms due to heat, but avoid direct sun or hot tubs if you find you react to them.

Medication

There are several ways that medication can worsen symptoms. If you're taking many drugs and they interact poorly, talk to your doctor. They can decide which drugs are vital and which ones you may be able to stop taking. Some people stop taking their MS medications because they have too many side effects or they believe they aren't effective. However, these medicines are critical to help prevent relapses and new lesions, so it's important to stay on them.

Lack of sleep

Fatigue is a common symptom of MS. If you're not getting enough sleep, this can decrease your energy even more.

Infections

From urinary tract infections to the cold or flu, infections can cause your symptoms to worsen. In fact, infections cause approximately one-third of all flare-ups of MS symptoms, according to the Cleveland Clinic.

Tests For Multiple Sclerosis

Multiple sclerosis can be difficult to diagnosis; there is no single test that can diagnose it. Instead, a diagnosis typically requires multiple tests to rule out other conditions with similar symptoms. After your doctor conducts a physical examination, they'll likely order several different tests if they suspect you may have MS.

Blood tests

Blood tests will likely be part of the initial workup if your doctor suspects you might have MS. Blood tests can't currently result in a firm diagnosis of MS, but they can rule out other conditions. These conditions include:

• Lyme disease
• rare hereditary disorders
• syphilis
• HIV/AIDS

All of these disorders can be diagnosed with bloodwork alone. Blood tests can also reveal abnormal results. This can lead toward diagnoses such as cancer or a vitamin B-12 deficiency.

Magnetic resonance imaging

Magnetic resonance imaging (MRI) is the test of choice for diagnosing MS in combination with initial blood tests. MRIs use radio waves and magnetic fields to evaluate the relative water content in tissues of the body. They can detect normal and abnormal tissues and can spot irregularities. MRIs offer detailed and sensitive images of the brain and spinal cord. They're much less invasive than X-rays or CT scans, which both use radiation.

Purpose: Doctors will be looking for two things when they order an MRI with a suspected diagnosis of MS. The first is that they'll check for any other abnormalities that could rule out MS and point to a different diagnosis, such as a brain tumor. They'll also look for evidence of demyelination. The layer of myelin that protects the nerve fibers is fatty and repels water when it's undamaged. If the myelin has been damaged, however, this fat content is reduced or stripped away entirely and no longer repels water. The area will hold more water as a result, which can be detected by MRIs. To diagnose MS, doctors must find evidence of demyelination. In addition to ruling out other potential conditions, an MRI can provide solid evidence that demyelination has occurred.

Preparation: Before you go in for your MRI, remove all jewelry. If you have any metal on your clothes (including zippers or bra hooks), you'll be asked to change into a hospital gown. You'll lie still inside the MRI machine (which is open on both ends) for the duration of the procedure, which takes between 45 minutes and 1 hour. Let your doctor and technician know ahead of time if you have:
• metallic implants
• pacemaker
• tattoos
• implanted drug infusions
• artificial heart valves
• history of diabetes
• any other conditions that you think could be relevant

Lumbar puncture

Lumbar puncture, also called a spinal tap, is sometimes used in the process of diagnosing MS. This procedure will remove a sample of the cerebrospinal fluid (CSF) for testing. Lumbar punctures are considered invasive. During the procedure, a needle is inserted into the lower back, between vertebrae, and into the spinal canal. This hollow needle will collect the sample of CSF for testing. A spinal tap typically takes about 30 minutes, and you will be given a local anesthetic. The patient is typically asked to lay on their side with their spine curved. After the area has been cleaned and a local anesthetic has been administered, a doctor will inject the hollow needle into the spinal canal to withdraw one to two tablespoons of CSF. Usually, there is no special preparation. You may be asked to stop taking blood thinners. Doctors who order lumbar punctures during the process of an MS diagnosis will use the test to rule out conditions with similar symptoms. They'll also look for signs of MS, specifically:

• elevated levels of antibodies called IgG antibodies
• proteins called oligoclonal bands
• an unusually high amount of white blood cells

The number of white blood cells in the spinal fluid of people with MS can be up to seven times higher than normal. However, these abnormal immune responses can also be caused by other conditions. It's also estimated that 5 to 10 percent of people with MS do not show any abnormalities in their CSF.

Evoked potential test

Evoked potential (EP) tests measure the electrical activity in the brain that occurs in response to stimulation, such as sound, touch, or sight. Each type of stimuli evokes minute electrical signals, which can be measured by the electrodes placed on the scalp to monitor activity in certain areas of the brain. There are three types of EP tests. The visual evoked response (VER or VEP) is the one most commonly used to diagnose MS. When doctors order an EP test, they're going to look for impaired transmission that is present along the optic nerve pathways. This typically happens fairly early in most MS patients. However, before concluding that abnormal VERs are due to MS, other ocular or retinal disorders must be excluded. No preparation is necessary to take an EP test. During the test, you'll sit in front of a screen that has an alternating checkerboard pattern on it. You may be asked to cover one eye at a time. It does require active concentration, but it's safe and noninvasive. If you wear glasses, ask your doctor ahead of time if you should bring them.

New tests under development

Medical knowledge is always advancing. As technology and our knowledge of MS moves forward, doctors may find new tests to make the MS diagnosis process an easier one. A blood test is currently being developed that will be able to detect biomarkers that are associated with MS. While this test likely won't be able to diagnose MS on its own, it can help doctors evaluate risk factors and make diagnosis just a little easier.

Diagnostic criteria

Doctors may have to repeat diagnostic tests for MS several times before they can confirm the diagnosis. This is because MS symptoms can change. They may diagnose someone with MS if testing points to the following criteria:

- Signs and symptoms indicate there's damage to the myelin in the CNS.
- The doctor has identified at least two or more lesions in two or more parts of the CNS via an MRI.
- There's evidence based on a physical exam that the CNS has been affected.
- A person has had two or more episodes of affected neurological function for at least one day, and they occurred a month apart. Or, a person's symptoms have progressed over the course of one year.
- The doctor can't find any other explanation for the person's symptoms.

Diagnostic criteria have changed over the years and will likely continue to change as new technology and research comes along. The most recent accepted criteria were published in 2017 as the revised McDonald Criteria. The International Panel on the Diagnosis of Multiple Sclerosis released these criteria. One of the more recent innovations in diagnosing MS is a tool called optical coherence tomography (OCT). This tool allows a doctor to obtain images of a person's optical nerve. The test is painless and is much like taking a picture of your eye. Doctors know that people with MS tend to have optic nerves that look different from people who don't have the disease. OCT also allows a doctor to track a person's eye health by looking at the optic nerve.

Multiple Sclerosis (MS) Treatments

While there's no cure for multiple sclerosis (MS), there are many treatments available. These treatments mainly focus on slowing down the progression of the disease and managing symptoms. Different people can have different types of MS. And disease progression and symptoms range greatly from person to person. For both reasons, each person's treatment plan will be different.

Disease-modifying drugs

Disease-modifying medications can reduce the frequency and severity of MS episodes, or relapses. They also can control the growth of lesions (damage to nerve fibers) and reduce symptoms. There are currently several drugs approved by the Food and Drug Administration (FDA) for modifying MS.

They come as injectables, infusions, and oral treatments.

Injectables: These four medications are given as injections:
- interferon beta-1a (Avonex, Rebif)
- interferon beta-1b (Betaseron, Extavia)
- glatiramer acetate (Copaxone, generic versions such as Glatopa)
- pegylated interferon beta-1a (Plegridy)

In 2018, the manufacturers of the injection daclizumab (Zinbryta) withdrew it from the market due to safety concerns.

Infusions: These four therapies must be given by infusion at a licensed clinic:
- alemtuzumab (Lemtrada)
- mitoxantrone (Novantrone)
- natalizumab (Tysabri)
- ocrelizumab (Ocrevus)

Oral treatments: These five treatments you take by mouth as pills:
- teriflunomide (Aubagio)
- fingolimod (Gilenya)

- dimethyl fumarate (Tecfidera)
- cladribine (Mavenclad)
- siponimod (Mayzent)

Treatments for relapses

Ending a relapse as quickly as possible benefits both the body and the mind. That's where relapse treatments come in.

Corticosteroids: Inflammation is a key feature of MS relapses. It can lead to many other symptoms of MS, such as:

- fatigue
- weakness
- pain

Corticosteroids are often used to ease inflammation and reduce the severity of MS attacks.Corticosteroids used to treat MS include methylprednisolone (intravenous) and prednisone (oral).

Other treatments: If corticosteroids don't provide relief for relapses, or if intravenous treatments can't be used, there are other treatments. These may include:

- ACTH (H.P. Acthar Gel): ACTH is an injection into your muscle or under your skin. It works by prompting the adrenal cortex gland to secrete the hormones cortisol, corticosterone, and aldosterone. These hormones reduce the level of inflammation in your body.
- Plasmapheresis: This processinvolves removing whole blood from your body and filtering it to remove antibodies that may be attacking your nervous system. The "cleansed" blood is then given back to you as a transfusion.
- Intravenous immunoglobulin (IVIG): This treatment is an injection that helps to boost your immune system. However, evidence of its benefits for MS relapses has been inconsistent in clinical studies.

Medications for physical symptoms

While the drugs listed above help treat MS, a range of medications are available to treat the different physical symptoms that MS can cause.

Drugs for pain and other muscle problems: Muscle relaxants are often prescribed for people with MS.

That's because relaxing muscles helps with common MS symptoms such as:
- pain
- muscle spasms
- fatigue

Relieving those symptoms can also help with depression, which can occur with MS. Drugs for muscle stiffness include:
- baclofen (Lioresal)
- cyclobenzaprine (Flexeril)
- diazepam (Valium)
- tizanidine (Zanaflex)

Drugs for fatigue: Fatigue is a common symptom for people with MS. Drugs used to treat fatigue include modafinil (Provigil). They also include amantadine hydrochloride (Gocovri), which is used off-label for this purpose. Off-label use is when a drug that's approved for one purpose is used for another. Fluoxetine (Prozac) is also often prescribed since it helps combat both fatigue and depression.

Drugs for bladder and bowel problems: There are more than a dozen prescription medications for bladder problems (such as incontinence) related to MS. Talk to your doctor about which drugs might be best for you. The most effective medications for constipation and bowel symptoms associated with MS seem to be over-the-counter stool softeners. If you have questions about these products, ask your pharmacist.

Exercise and physical therapy

Constant movement and activity are critical to fighting MS. Exercise helps:
- improve muscle strength
- increase cardiovascular health
- improve mood
- improve cognitive function

However, people with MS often experience fatigue. And when you're tired, you may not feel like exercising. But the less exercise you get, the more tired you'll feel. That's another reason why exercise, including physical therapy (PT), is so important. However, it needs to be carefully tailored to people with MS. Things such as keeping session times short and increasing exercise over time are important factors.

When to seek PT: Someone with MS should consider PT during a relapse that has produced a change in functions such as:
- walking
- coordination
- strength
- energy

The goal of PT during relapse is to return to a prior level of function, if possible.

Benefits of PT: A professional PT program will help improve your strength and physical function. It may also include self-care activities such as:
- home exercise programs
- aqua therapy
- yoga
- a personal fitness program at a gym or health club

Getting out of the house to exercise has the bonus of helping to address depression and social isolation that people with MS can experience.

Where to begin: A good way to start your MS exercise routine is to try basic stretches while you're sitting or in bed. When you feel comfortable with those exercises, add more demanding exercises such as walking, water exercise, or dancing. As you get stronger and more comfortable exercising, you can modify and build on your exercise program. Keep in mind that anything you can do with others, especially exercise you enjoy, can help.

Managing emotions during change

If you have MS, physical symptoms aren't the only things you have to deal with. You may face a constantly changing illness, which can make coping with your condition emotionally challenging. You might feel symptoms that include:

• depression
• grief
• emotional instability
• anger

Two popular treatment options are medication and therapy. But while antidepressants can often help relieve symptoms, they may not be enough. And although talk therapy with a licensed practitioner is a good idea, you may need help from someone who has a more personal understanding of MS. Your next step might be to find someone to talk to who understands what you're going through. Look to your local MS Society for education, counseling references, and support groups. Talking with people who know what it means to have MS can provide you with coping strategies and remind you that you're not the only one dealing with this condition.

Living With MS

Most people with MS find ways to manage their symptoms and function well.

Medications

Having MS means you'll need to see a doctor experienced in treating MS. If you take one of the DMTs, you'll have to make sure you adhere to the recommended schedule. Your doctor may prescribe other medications to treat specific symptoms.

Diet and exercise

A well-balanced diet, low in empty calories and high in nutrients and fiber, will help you manage your overall health. Regular exercise is important for physical and mental health, even if you have disabilities. If physical movement is difficult, swimming or exercising in a swimming pool can help. Some yoga classes are designed just for people with MS.

Other complementary therapies

Studies regarding the effectiveness of complementary therapies are scarce, but that doesn't mean they can't help in some way. The following may help you feel less stressed and more relaxed:

- meditation
- massage
- tai chi
- acupuncture
- hypnotherapy
- music therapy

Effects Of MS

The lesions from MS can appear anywhere in your CNS and affect any part of your body.

Mobility issues

As you age, some disabilities from MS may become more pronounced. If you have mobility issues, falling may put you at an increased risk of bone fractures. Having other conditions such as arthritis and osteoporosis can complicate matters.

Other issues

One of the most common symptoms of MS is fatigue, but it's not uncommon for people with MS to also have:

- depression
- anxiety
- some degree of cognitive impairment

Prognosis For People With MS

It's almost impossible to predict how MS will progress in any one person. About 10 to 15 percent of people with MS have only rare attacks and minimal disability ten years after diagnosis. This is sometimes called benign MS. About half of people with MS use a cane or other form of assistance 15 years after receiving an MS diagnosis. At 20 years, about 60 percent are still ambulatory and less than 15 percent need care for their basic needs.

MS type

Progressive MS generally advances faster than RRMS. People with RRMS can be in remission for many years. A lack of disability after five years is usually a good indicator for the future.

Age and sex

The disease generally progresses faster in men than in women. It may also progress faster in those who receive a diagnosis after age 40 and in those who have a high relapse rate.

MS and Diet

If you have multiple sclerosis (MS), you've probably heard conflicting claims about a new diet or supplement that could help your symptoms. More studies are now being done to examine how nutrition can impact people living with MS. However, many results have been conflicting or inconclusive. Some diet plans can jeopardize your health and omit nutrients. So, eating a well-balanced, low-fat diet full of fiber and colorful fruits and vegetables is likely the best place to start.

Talk with your doctor to find out the facts before starting any diet plan.

Low fat for good health

According to the National Multiple Sclerosis Society, many neurologists recommend a low-fat, high-fiber diet to maintain optimal health. This includes avoiding saturated fats and trans fats, and eating healthy mono- and polyunsaturated fats such as those found in olive oil, nuts, and avocados. Unsaturated fats are important building blocks of myelin and nervous system tissue. Keep in mind that moderation is the key. Less than 30 percent of daily calories should come from any kind of fat.

Swank diet has mixed results

In the 1980s, Dr. Roy Swank developed a very strict, low-fat diet for people with MS. In the Swank diet, fats are restricted. Fish oils are allowed. According to the Swank MS Foundation, overall calories from fat should be less than 30 percent of daily intake — a maximum of 65 grams of total fat per day. In a 1990 article in the Lancet, Swank's research group reported that people with MS who followed his diet saw less deterioration and lower mortality rates. However, some researchers aren't convinced there's enough current data to back up his claims. Studies are ongoing to determine if the Swank diet or other extremely low-fat diets have significant benefits for people with MS.

PUFA

Several studies have shown that increasing intake of polyunsaturated fatty acids (PUFAs) may help people with MS. These unsaturated fats have anti-inflammatory effects in animal studies. Linoleic acid, an omega-6 fatty acid, in combination with other nutrients including omega-3 fatty acids, decreased relapse rates and slowed disease progression in a clinical trial. However, other studies show no effect. Overall, researchers are not yet sure if it's worthwhile to add supplementation with PUFAs to an MS treatment regimen. Studies are inconclusive, and research is ongoing.

Vitamin D

Research published in the Journal of the Academy of Nutrition and Dietetics indicates that sufficient vitamin D levels may prevent the development of autoimmune diseases like MS. Research published in the Journal of Therapeutic Advances in Neurological Disorders suggests that vitamin D can also influence relapse rate and the number of lesions seen on MRIs. However, more studies are needed for conclusive evidence. Many neurologists recommend supplementation if blood levels are low. Recommended daily intake of vitamin D is 600 IU for adults (not to exceed 4000 IU per day). For patients with very low vitamin D levels, doctors may recommend taking more than that for a few months to bring vitamin D levels back to normal. However, too much vitamin D can be toxic, so it's important to speak with your doctor before taking any supplements.

Gluten

The effects of a gluten-free diet on MS are conflicting. Research from Israel suggests that some people with MS also have antibodies that are normally associated with celiac disease, a digestive disorder caused by an abnormal immune reaction to gluten. Gluten is a protein found in wheat and some other grains. The presence of these antibodies suggests a link between immune intolerance to gluten and autoimmune diseases like MS. However, other research findings and some neurologists suggest that there is no link between gluten antibodies and MS. More studies need to be done to draw any solid conclusions.

Antioxidants

Free radicals do some of the damage that occurs during the formation of MS lesions. Free radicals cause oxidative stress, and can be neutralized by antioxidants like vitamins A, C, E, beta carotene, lutein, lycopene, and selenium. A study in 2015 revealed that people with MS had significantly lower antioxidant levels and higher oxidative stress in their saliva. Chronic inflammation during an attack can cause deficiencies in antioxidant levels in the body. Supplementation may restore levels of these key nutrients. However, high doses may have other effects, not yet been studied on people with MS.

Ongoing research

Researchers are looking into the role that nutrition can play in treating MS, but many questions remain. Vitamin D shows promise in slowing the progression of MS. Omega-3 and omega-6 fatty acids may be valuable in protecting nerve health. Antioxidants and other nutrients like probiotics may also play valuable roles in a treatment regimen. How the gut microbiome (intestinal bacteria population) affects neurodegenerative diseases is a new frontier in research. Early research shows that improving gut bacteria can reduce the risk of gut permeability. It may also improve symptoms of MS and slow the progression of the disease. For now, a diet low in fat, high in fiber, and rich in plant foods — fruits, vegetables, and whole grains — seems to be the most evidence-based diet for the best long-term health of a person living with MS. However, there's not enough evidence yet to show clear benefits of their use.

Multiple Sclerosis Diet
The Role Of Good Nutrition

Eating healthy, nutritious food is an important part of feeling well and managing symptoms of multiple sclerosis (MS). In MS, the immune system attacks the central nervous system, blocking or interrupting nerve signals and causing symptoms such as:
- fatigue
- numbness
- movement problems
- bladder and bowel dysfunction
- vision problems

Your diet is an important tool when it comes to living well with these symptoms.

Foods To Eat

Certain foods may benefit people with MS by affecting how the immune system, the nerves, and other parts of the body work.

Probiotics and prebiotics

Changes in gut health may contribute to immune disorders, and research indicates that the health of the gut appears to play a role in many kinds of diseases. The intestinal flora, or gut flora, is a highly complex system of microorganisms that live in the intestines. In humans, these microorganisms are largely bacteria. The bacteria are responsible for breaking down food and nutrients, and they play a key role in digestion and the health of the immune system. Healthy gut flora thrive in the intestines when there is ample fiber in the diet. A lack of healthy gut flora may contribute to a range of immune disorders, including MS. Anyone with the condition should have a diet that supports a healthy immune system, and one that promotes beneficial gut flora may help. Probiotics are foods that can boost levels of beneficial bacteria in the gut, helping to strengthen the immune system. The authors of a study in Nature Communications suggest that adjusting the gut flora, by using probiotics, for example, may be helpful for people with MS. Probiotic bacteria are available in supplements and a range of fermented foods. The following all contain healthful levels of Lactobacillus, which is one type of beneficial bacteria:

• yogurt
• kefir

- kimchi
- sauerkraut
- kombucha, or fermented tea

Prebiotics: After filling the gut with good bacteria, it is important to feed them. Foods that nourish probiotic bacteria are called prebiotics, and they contain fiber. Foods that contain healthful levels of prebiotic fiber include:

- artichokes
- garlic
- leeks
- asparagus
- onions
- chicory

Fiber

Fiber occurs in plant-based foods, such as:

- fruits
- vegetables
- nuts and seeds
- legumes, such as lentils
- whole grains
- brown rice

It helps promote health in the following ways:
- nourishing the gut bacteria
- encouraging regular bowel movements
- keeping blood pressure and the heart healthy by helping manage cholesterol
- reducing the risk of weight gain by leaving a person feeling full for longer

People with MS may have a higher risk of certain types of heart disease. While dietary measures may not reduce these risks, a healthful diet will benefit overall heart health.

Vitamin D

Vitamin D is important for everyone, but it may be especially beneficial for people with MS. According to the National Institute of Neurological Disorders and Stroke, people with high levels of vitamin D appear to have a lower chance of developing MS. Vitamin D is also important for bone health. People with MS may be more likely to experience low bone density and osteoporosis, especially if they are not able to move easily. An adequate intake of vitamin D may help prevent this. Most of the body's

vitamin D comes from exposure to sunlight, but a person also takes it in by consuming:
- oily fish
- fortified dairy products
- some fortified cereals, yogurt, and orange juice
- beef liver
- egg yolks

A review published in 2017 notes that, while evidence of a link between low vitamin D levels and MS is accumulating, confirming the link will require more research.

Biotin

Biotin is a form of vitamin B, and some people call it vitamin H. It occurs in many foods, but good sources include:
- eggs
- yeast
- beef liver
- sunflower seeds
- almonds
- spinach
- broccoli

- whole-wheat bread

Researchers have been looking into whether biotin might benefit people with MS. Findings from small studies indicate that a high dosage of biotin — between 100 and 600 milligrams per day — could help people with progressive MS, in which symptoms gradually become more severe. Confirming and specifying the benefits of biotin supplementation will require more research, but following a healthful diet can often ensure that a person is consuming enough of this vitamin.

Polyunsaturated fatty acids

Investigations into whether a diet rich in polyunsaturated fatty acids (PUFAs) directly helps relieve MS symptoms have yielded mixed results. However, there is evidence that these acids help support a healthy body and control inflammation. A study published in 2017 concluded that a low intake of PUFAs may increase the risk of MS. The study looked at data from more than 170,000 women. PUFAs appear to boost bodily functions ranging from cardiac health to the ability to think. Examples of foods that contain PUFAs include fatty fish, such as salmon and mackerel, and some plant-based oils.

Antioxidants

Many vegetable-based foods contain substances called polyphenols, which have antioxidant and anti-inflammatory effects on the body's cells. These effects may help prevent cell damage, making polyphenols potentially useful for people with MS. Sources of polyphenols include:

- fruits
- vegetables
- spices
- cereals
- legumes
- fruits
- herbs
- tea

Antioxidants can also help prevent oxidative stress, which researchers have linked to a wide range of health problems. Some antioxidants — specifically resveratrol, which occurs in grapes — appear to help protect the nervous system.

Foods To Avoid

Limit saturated fats

Physician Roy Swank introduced his low-fat diet for MS in 1948. He claimed that saturated fats in animal products and tropical oils worsen MS symptoms. Swank's research is controversial. It was conducted before MRIs could measure the progression of MS, and his studies lacked a control group. Nevertheless, reducing your saturated fat intake to less than 15 grams a day makes sense for your overall health. It's a positive, healthy step toward good health. However, don't eliminate all fats. Unsaturated fatty acids are important for brain and cellular health. They contain omega-3s, and vitamin D which may have a protective effect on MS. Foods that have vitamin D and omega-3s include fatty fish such as salmon, tuna, and mackerel. An analysis of the Nurses' Health Study (I and II) failed to show a link between fat consumption and development of MS. A theoretical connection between dairy sensitivity and the number and severity of MS flare-ups also hasn't been proven by research. Dairy should be avoided by anyone who is intolerant of it. Opting for a diet low in saturated and trans-fat is another protective strategy that may improve your overall health.

Drop the diet drinks

Drinks with aspartame, caffeine, and alcohol can irritate the bladder. According to nutritional guidelines from National Multiple Sclerosis Society (NMSS), it's best to stay away from these drinks if you have bladder-related MS symptoms. But you don't have to worry about aspartame causing MS, that's a myth.

Gluten

A study published in BMC Neurology reported that selected MS patients and their immediate family members had a higher incidence of gluten intolerance than the general population. But that doesn't mean all MS patients should go gluten-free. The decision to shift to a gluten-free diet, which eliminates all wheat, rye, barley, and triticale foods, should be made on a case-by-case basis. The researchers also recommended early detection and treatment of gluten intolerance for MS patients.

Fruit instead of refined sugars

No scientific evidence shows that refined sugars are linked to MS flare-ups. However, refined and processed sugar is highly inflammatory and should be limited. In addition, going easy on sweet foods helps you manage your weight, which is very important for people with MS. Sugar- and calorie-laden foods can pack on pounds, and extra weight can increase MS-related fatigue. Being overweight also may contribute to mobility problems and raise cardiovascular disease risk. The occasional slice of birthday cake is fine, but generally choose fruit as your snack and dessert option. High-fiber fruit also helps ease constipation, another MS symptom.

Special Diets

Anyone on a specific diet needs to be sure that they are consuming all the required daily nutrients. A person who eliminates a particular food or food group should ensure that they replace any nutrients lost.

Gluten-free diet

Research has not confirmed a link between gluten and MS, but people with MS appear to have a higher likelihood of developing celiac disease, which prevents the body from tolerating gluten. Both diseases seem to stem from a problem with the immune system. Foods that contain gluten include:

• wheat products, such as breads, baked goods, and many premade soups and salad dressings

• barley products, such as malt, soups, beer, and brewer's yeast

• rye, which is often present in bread, rye beer, and cereals

People who follow a gluten-free diet may miss out on important nutrients, including fiber, which is present in whole grains. They should boost their fiber intake by eating plenty of fresh vegetables, fruits, nuts, seeds, and pulses. Anyone considering a gluten-free diet should speak to their doctor first.

Paleo diet

Many people on the Paleo, or Paleolithic, diet believe that the human body has not evolved to eat the highly processed foods that we now consume.

The diet involves switching to foods that were likely eaten by hunter-gatherers. The first step is to choose natural foods over processed foods, with an emphasis on meat and plant-based foods, but not grains. In a 2019 review, researchers, including an advocate of the Paleo diet, compared a modified version of it with another diet — the Swank diet — to test, among other factors, the effects on MS-related fatigue. There is some evidence that the diets may reduce this fatigue, but confirming this will require more research.

Swank diet

Doctors developed the Swank diet as an MS treatment in the 1950s. It reduces saturated fat intake to, at most, 15 grams per day and recommends limiting unsaturated fat intake to 20–50 grams per day. People on this diet:

- cannot eat processed foods or dairy fats
- cannot eat red meat, during the first year
- can eat as much white fish and shellfish as they like

- should eat at least 2 cups each of fruits and vegetables every day
- should eat whole-grain pasta
- should take cod liver oil and multivitamins every day

While some consider the diet to be dated, others report that it helps. Possible risks include deficiencies in folic acid and vitamins A, C, and E.

Recipes

Roasted Chicken Breast With Garlic Cloves

serves 4

Ingredients

- Four 6-ounces chicken breasts with bones and skin
- 8 to 10 garlic cloves
- 4 teaspoons olive oil
- 1 tablespoon dried Italian herb
- 1 large lemon, cut in 8 slices
- 2 pinches of coarse salt
- Pepper to taste
- Serve with steamed vegetables and lemon wedges.

Cooking instructions

- Preheat the oven to 375 °F. Mince the garlic cloves on a clean cutting board. Sprinkle the coarse salt over the minced garlic cloves. Press with the side of a chef's knife until you end up with smooth paste. Transfer to a bowl. Mix in the olive oil, Italian herbs, and season with pepper. With your fingers, carefully separate the chicken skin slightly from the flesh, being careful not to break the skin. Spread the garlic mixture over the chicken flesh, add 2 lemon slices per breast, and push back the skin. Place the breasts in a baking dish and bake for 20 to 25 minutes, or until cooked through. Time may vary depending on the thickness of the breasts. Serve immediately and disregard skin when eating.

Bell Peppers And Turkey Roll

serves 1

Ingredients

- ½ medium yellow squash, cut into strips (about 3 ounces)
- ½ medium bell pepper, seeded, ribs removed, and cut into strips (about 3 ounces)
- 1 tablespoon sun-dried tomatoes, minced

- 3 ounces turkey slices (about 1 ounce each or 3 slices)
- 3 tablespoons eggplant spread
- 6 basil leaves
- Salt and pepper to taste

You may substitute eggplant spread with hummus. This may be served with a small salad on the side for a light lunch meal.

Cooking instructions

- Mix the sun-dried tomatoes and eggplant spread in a bowl. Lay each turkey slice on a large cutting board. Spread 1 tablespoon of the prepared mixture and 2 basil leaves over each turkey slice. Divide the bell pepper and zucchini strips equally on top of each turkey slice, and season to taste. Roll up each turkey slice and serve immediately.

Wild Smoked Salmon Roll

serves 1

Ingredients

- 3 ounces smoked salmon (about 4 slices)
- 12 asparagus, trimmed (about 12 ounces asparagus)

- 4 tablespoons Boursin light cheese
- Pepper to taste

This may be served with a small salad on the side for a light lunch meal.

Cooking Instructions

- Preheat a steamer over high heat. Add the asparagus, reduce heat, and cook until desired doneness. Remove from the steamer and blanch in ice-cold water to stop the cooking process. Lay each smoked salmon slice on a large cutting board. Spread 1 tablespoon of Boursin over each slice. Add 3 asparagus per slice, sprinkle with pepper to taste, and roll. Serve immediately or refrigerate until needed.

Radishes With Hazelnut Sour Cream

serves 4

Ingredients

- 10 radishes
- 1 tablespoon low-fat sour cream
- 1 teaspoon low-fat milk
- 1 tablespoon hazelnuts
- Pinch of salt

- Pinch of pepper

Mix in a little horseradish or fine herbs. You may substitute low-fat sour cream with low-fat yogurt.

Cooking instructions

- Crush and mince the hazelnuts with a chef knife. Mix the sour cream with the milk in a bowl. Add the minced hazelnuts, salt, and pepper. Serve immediately with the radishes.

Apple And Almond Butter

serves 1

Ingredients

- 1 small apple (about 4 ounces)
- 1 tablespoon almond butter

Cooking instructions

- Cut the apple in half, remove core, and slice. Equally spread the almond butter among the slices.

Cottage Cheese, Raisins, And Walnuts

serves 1

Ingredients

- ⅓ cup low-fat cottage cheese, cold
- 1 tablespoon chopped walnuts
- 2 teaspoons raisins

- Cinnamon to taste

Cooking instructions

- Mix cottage cheese, walnut, and raisins. Sprinkle with cinnamon to taste and serve immediately.

Sardines With Edamame

serves 2

Ingredients

- 1 can sardines (about 4 ¼ ounces)
- ½ cup cooked Edamame
- ¼ lemon, juiced
- Salt and pepper to taste

Cooking instructions

- Roughly chop the sardines in a bowl. Mix in the Edamame and lemon juice. Season to taste and serve immediately.

Apple And Pear Minestrone

serves 2

Ingredients

- 1 medium apple, brunoise (about 5 ounces)
- 1 medium pear, brunoise (about 5 ounces)
- ¾ cup jasmine green tea (or your favorite)
- 1 ½ teaspoon honey

- ½ teaspoon pumpkin pie spices
- 1 small ginger root, minced
- ½ teaspoon lemon zest
- ½ teaspoon grapeseed oil

Cooking instructions

- Heat the oil in a deep saucepan over high heat. Add the apple and sauté for two minutes. Add the pear, spices, ginger, lemon zest, and sauté another minute. Add the green tea and bring to a boil. Remove from heat and transfer to a serving bowl. Cool at room temperature. Refrigerate for an hour or, even better, overnight to allow flavors to emerge. Serve cold.

Baked Apples With Cranberries

serves 4; 1 serving: 1 apple

Ingredients

- 4 large apples
- 3 tablespoons red currant jelly
- 4 tablespoons cranberry juice
- 4 teaspoons walnuts
- 4 teaspoons cranberries

Cooking instructions

- Preheat the oven to 400 degrees F.
- Wash and core the apples, being careful not to break through the bottom of the apples. Place them in a baking pan that is just the right size to keep the apples close to each other. Put 1 teaspoon of red currant jelly in the cavity of each apple. Pour one tablespoon of cranberry juice over the cavity of each apple.
- Add a little hot water in the pan (¼ inch). Cover the pan with aluminum foil and bake for 20 minutes. Remove cover and baste with the liquid in the pan. Continue baking uncovered for 4 to 5 minutes. If necessary, add a little more water to avoid burning.
- Place each apple in a serving dish. Scrape particles from the pan and transfer the liquid to a saucepan. Blend the liquid with the remaining red currant jelly and bring to a boil over high heat. Pour over the apples, sprinkle with the walnuts, cranberries, and serve immediately.

Acai And Almond Milk Popsicle
serves 4

Ingredients

- 3.5 ounces Pure Acai, no sugar added
- 4 ounces berries (about 1 cup)
- 1 small banana (about 4 ounces)
- 4 ounces almond milk

Option: You may substitute almond milk with soy milk or low-fat milk.

Cooking instructions

- Place all the fruits and almond milk in a blender. Purée on high speed. Divide equally among 4 popsicles maker and freeze.

Red Fruits Compote

serves 4

Ingredients

- 8 ounces blackberries
- 8 ounces raspberries
- 8 ounces blueberries
- 8 ounces strawberries
- 3 tablespoons honey
- 1 large organic lemon peel
- 1 large organic orange peel
- 1 cup pomegranate juice (no sugar added)

- Cornstarch and water

Suggestion: Serve with low-fat yogurt, sherbet, cream of millet, apple slices, etc.

Cooking instructions

- Wash the berries and carefully pat dry. Place the pomegranate juice in a saucepan and bring to boil over high heat. Reduce by half. If necessary, thicken with a little water-cornstarch mixture. Add the honey, berries, and cook for a minute or two.
- Do not overcook, or you will end up with a sauce rather than a compote. Remove from heat and transfer the compote to a bowl. Place the bowl in an ice-cold water bath to stop the cooking process. Refrigerate for two hours before serving.

Grilled Mango And Almonds

serves 4

Ingredients

- 4 mangos, slightly firm, peeled and thickly sliced
- 4 tablespoons sliced almonds
- 4 teaspoons honey
- 1 orange, juiced

Cooking instructions

- Preheat the broiler. Cover the bottom of a baking sheet with parchment paper. Add the sliced almonds and broil until slightly browned. Remove the almonds from the sheet and cool.
- Cover the bottom of a baking sheet with parchment paper. Add the mango slices and broil until slightly browned. Meanwhile heat the honey with the orange juice in a pan and bring to a boil. Divide the mango slices among four plates.Drizzle with the warm sauce, sprinkle with the sliced almonds, and serve immediately.

Peach With Apricot Coulis

serves 4

Ingredients

- 4 peaches
- 12 apricots
- 1 tablespoon honey
- 1 teaspoon lemon juice
- 1 rosemary branch
- 4 teaspoons almonds

Cooking instructions

• Cut apricots in half and remove pits. Place the apricots in a pan.

• Add ½ cup water, honey, rosemary, lemon juice, and bring to a boil. Reduce heat, cover, and simmer for ten minutes. Purée in a blender and transfer to a serving bowl. Let cool and refrigerate. Peel and cut the peaches in half. Place the peach halves in a serving platter, drizzle with some apricot sauce and the almonds. Serve with the remaining apricot sauce on the side.

Strawberries And Spinach Smoothie

serves 2

Ingredients

• 2 cups strawberries (about 10 ounces)

• 1 bunch fresh spinach

• 1 banana

• 1 tablespoon flaxseeds Aged balsamic vinegar to taste (optional)

• Ice cubes

Cooking instructions

- Place strawberries, spinach, and banana in a blender. Puree and mix in the aged balsamic vinegar (optional). Serve immediately.

Spring Fruit Salad With White Tea

serves 4

Ingredients
- 1 small banana, sliced
- 3 ounces strawberries, halved
- 3 ounces blueberries
- 3 ounces raspberries
- 1 small apple, cubed
- 2 large plums, quartered
- 1 white tea sachet
- 1 tablespoon honey
- 1 tablespoon lemon juice

Cooking instructions
- Boil ¾ cup of water. Add the lemon juice, tea sachet, honey, and infuse until desired strength.Remove sachet and cool completely. Blend all the fruits in a large bowl. Add the cold tea and refrigerate for 30 minutes, mixing every 10 minutes. Serve cold.

Winter Fruit Salad
>serves 4
>
>Ingredients
>- 1 small banana, sliced
>- 1 pear, diced
>- 1 apple, diced
>- 6 ounces grapes
>- 1 orange, peeled and segmented
>- ¼ cup pomegranate seeds
>- 2 tablespoons lemon juice
>
>Cooking instructions
>- Blend all the fruits in a large bowl. Mix in the lemon juice, pomegranate seeds, and refrigerate until use.

Melon Soup
>serves 4
>
>Ingredients
>- 2 cantaloupes (or 4 cups)
>- 2 tablespoons honey (quickly warmed in the microwave)
>- 4 mint leaves
>- 1 lemon, juiced

Cooking instructions

- Cut the cantaloupes in half. Remove seeds. Spoon out the flesh and place in a blender. Add the honey, mint, and lemon juice. Purée and refrigerate. Serve cold.

Thin Peach And Apricot Tart

serves 8

Ingredients

- 3 ounces almond meal
- 2 ounces oats
- 3 tablespoons grapeseed oil
- Pinch of salt
- 1 tablespoon almond extract
- 2 to 3 tablespoons ice cold water
- 2 tablespoons apricot preserves
- 2 large peaches (about 8 ounces)
- 4 large apricots (about 8 ounces)

Cooking instructions

- Preheat the oven to 475°F. Place the oats in a blender and reduce to a flour consistency. Place the oat and almond flours in a bowl. Add salt, oil, almond extract, and mix until crumbly.

- Add one tablespoon water at a time and continue until the dough is smooth and sticks together as one ball.Lay the dough on wax paper and push down with your palm to flatten a bit.
- Roll out the dough to a round thin form. Then turn over the dough to a cookie sheet. Brush 1 tablespoon preserves all over the pie dough surface. Peel the peaches, apricots, and cut in half.Core, quarter, and slice. Starting at the edge of the dough and working inward toward the center, arrange the peach slices in overlapping circles. Finish with a circle of apricot slices in the center.Bake for 15 to 20 minutes until golden brown with slightly darker edges.Heat the remaining preserves in the microwave with a little water to thin. Remove the tart from the oven and brush with the peach preserves. Transfer to a cooling rack.

Printed in Great Britain
by Amazon